Clothes

Jon Richards

Chrysalis Children's Books

First published in the UK in 2004 by
Chrysalis Children's Books
An imprint of Chrysalis Books Group Plc
The Chrysalis Building, Bramley Road,
London W10 6SP

ISBN 1 84458 113 6

British Library Cataloguing in Publication Data for this
book is available from the British Library.

Editorial Manager *Joyce Bentley*
Editorial Assistant *Camilla Lloyd*
Produced by Tall Tree Ltd
Designer *Ed Simkins*
Editor *Kate Simkins*
Consultant *Jon Kirkwood*
Picture Researcher *Lorna Ainger*

Printed in China

Some of the more unfamiliar words used in this book
are explained in the glossary on page 31.

Typography *Natascha Frensch*
Read Regular, READ SMALLCAPS and Read Space;
European Community Design Registration 2003 and
Copyright © Natascha Frensch 2001-2004
Read Medium, Read Black and *Read Slanted*
Copyright © Natascha Frensch 2003-2004

READ™ is a revolutionary new typeface that will enchance
children's understanding through clear, easily recognisable
character shapes. With its evenly spaced and carefully
designed characters, READ™ will help children at all stages
to improve their literacy skills, and is ideal for young readers,
reluctant readers and especially children with dyslexia.

Contents

Natural fibres

The fibres used to make the earliest cloth by hand came from natural sources, including plants such as cotton and animals such as sheep. These natural materials are still widely worn today.

Sheep and their wool have been a source of material for thousands of years. Wool production is still an important industry, and some sheep farms are larger than small countries.

◄ After the wool has been shorn off a sheep, it is spun to form the wool yarn. This is then woven or knitted to produce cloth.

► Silk fibres are made by caterpillars called silkworms as they build cocoons. The cocoons are unwound to produce the silk fibres.

Silk was first made in China 5000 years ago. For centuries, the Chinese kept the method of silk production a secret, so that the material was expensive and much sought after. Even today, silk remains a luxury item.

LOOK CLOSER

Denim is a cloth named after the French town of Nîmes (*serge de Nîmes*, meaning 'cloth of Nîmes', was shortened to de *Nîmes* and then 'denim'). This tough cotton was an ideal choice for working clothes. In 1873, Levi Strauss used it to make jeans, which remain popular today.

Making cloth

In order to produce clothes, you need to weave, knit or squash fibres to make cloth. Cloth-making has been an important industry for hundreds of years and was one of the first to use powered machines in factories.

Weaving material on looms is the most common way of making cloth, and the earliest hand-operated looms are over 7000 years old. For many years, weaving was usually done by people in their homes.

◀ This image from the 19th century shows a Russian peasant weaving cloth on a small hand loom outside her home.

◄ Today, most cloth is woven on looms that are controlled by computer.

The Industrial Revolution, which started in England at the end of the 18th century, introduced powered machines that could produce cloth in large quantities. Weaving became based in factories surrounded by large towns that housed factory workers.

EUREKA!

The spinning jenny was invented by James Hargreaves in 1764. It could produce as much thread and yarn as several people for a fraction of the cost. Its introduction created protests and riots from people who were put out of work.

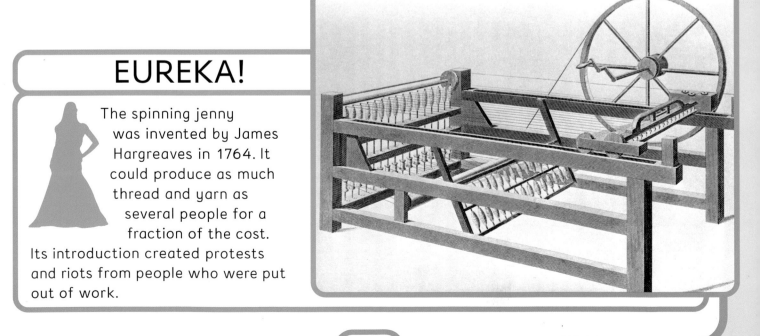

Artificial fibres

The invention of artificial fibres, such as nylon and rayon, has allowed manufacturers to create cheaper and more readily available alternatives to natural materials. Many of these fibres are ideal for special uses, such as sport.

The first artificial fibres appeared at the end of the 19th century. During World War II (1939–1945), these fibres were ideal substitutes for natural materials, such as silk, which were in short supply and expensive.

◄ Materials such as Lycra and neoprene are worn by sportsmen and women for improved aerodynamics.

Today, artificial fibres are easy to produce. This has decreased production time and, in many cases, reduced the cost of clothing. These fibres are also used to make clothes to suit specific activities, such as tight-fitting clothes for sprinters and warm, waterproof clothes for climbers.

◄ Climbers need clothes to keep them warm and dry in harsh conditions.

LOOK CLOSER

Nylon is an artificial material that was developed in the 1930s in the USA. Nylon fibres are produced by mixing certain chemical liquids together. The mixture forms a sticky substance that can be drawn into thin fibres. These fibres are perfect for weaving.

Colourful patterns

Colours and patterns were added to clothes to make them look more attractive or to show a person's status in a particular group or clan.

Early dyes provided a range of colours, but some were harder to produce than others. Purple, for example, was rare and very expensive. As a result, purple clothes in Ancient Rome were only worn by powerful people, such as the emperor. Early patterns were produced by weaving, creating simple crisscross patterns, or by printing onto materials.

◄ The purple dye used to colour the cloak of the Roman Emperor shown in this mosaic was produced by a difficult process using sea snails called murex.

Advances in printing and weaving have made patterned cloth easier to produce. Computerised looms weave fabric in a variety of patterns. Artificial dyes are used to create clothes in a vast range of colours.

◀ In tie-dying, knots are tied in the cloth to stop the dyes from colouring parts of the material.

LOOK CLOSER

Tartan is an old pattern that has stripes of crisscrossing colours. It is commonly linked to Scotland, UK, where it has been used for centuries to show the membership of a family, or clan. Each clan has its own pattern of tartan, using different colours and designs.

Skirts and dresses

A skirt is a tube of cloth that is worn to cover the legs. A dress combines a skirt with a bodice to cover the upper body. There are many styles of skirts and dresses, especially with the flexibility of modern fabrics.

References to skirts and dresses date back over 6000 years. People in Ancient Egypt wore a draped dress – a simple piece of cloth that was pulled over the head and gathered in with a belt.

◄ These Indian women are wearing a type of dress called a sari, which is a strip of cloth wound around the body. A short blouse called a choli is worn underneath.

The designs for skirts and dresses changed to reflect the fashions of the day. These fashions vary from the enormous skirts worn by women in 17th- and 18th-century Europe to modern figure-hugging designs.

▲ In the 18th century, the fashion was for wide dresses that were supported by many layers of undergarments.

LOOK CLOSER

For hundreds of years, women in Western countries have worn long skirts. In the 20th century, this changed as women gained more independence. The miniskirt was introduced in the 1960s. This was a very short skirt that was made popular by the famous fashion designer Mary Quant.

Formal suits

Suits for men were first worn in the 17th century. Since then their style and design have altered to reflect changes in fashion and society.

At first, the suit consisted of a long coat, underneath which was worn a vest, or waistcoat, and trousers called breeches that reached just below the knee. In the 19th century, long trousers were introduced to create the lounge suit, the forerunner of today's suit.

▼ These men from the 19th century show how it was fashionable for suits of the period to consist of items of different colours.

▲ All the items in a modern business suit are usually made from the same material.

Today, suits are worn as formal attire by both men and women. Women started to wear suits during the second half of the 19th century for pastimes such as cycling and riding. In the 20th century, as a reflection of the growing equality between the sexes, women started to wear trouser suits.

EUREKA!

Braces for holding up trousers were first used by the French in the 17th century but were made popular in the mid-18th century by the US inventor Benjamin Franklin. These early braces had an H-shaped back, but X- and Y-shaped backs were introduced later.

Underwear

What we wear beneath our outer clothes has many uses, from keeping us warm to altering our shape. Underwear has changed to suit different fashions and needs.

In ancient civilisations, people wore simple forms of underwear, such as the *schenti*, or loincloth, from Ancient Egypt. Those living in cold climates added more layers of underwear to stay warm. In Medieval Europe, both men and women wore a loose undershirt called a chemise and undershorts called braies.

◀ This woman is modelling hoops that were worn under dresses in the 18th and 19th centuries to create a wide skirt.

EUREKA!

Before the invention of the bra, women wore corsets (shown here). In 1893, Marie Tucek invented a 'breast supporter' that was similar to the modern bra. In 1913, Mary Phelps Jacob of New York, USA, made her own bra out of handkerchiefs and some ribbon. She was the first to patent, or register, the design with the US government.

PRICE ONLY 5/6 POST FREE

MAGNETIC CORSET

C.B.HARNESS

THEY CURE WEAK BAC

Women used to wear corsets to create a narrow waist. Layers of underskirts called petticoats made from stiff material, such as crinoline, gave women a fashionably full skirt. Today, comfort is as important as style. New materials such as Lycra have led to the creation of stretchy underwear that shapes the body but is comfortable to wear.

◄ Thermal underwear is made of a special material that retains the body's heat and keeps the wearer warm.

Headgear

Hats and headgear are worn by people to keep them warm, to protect the head, to show their rank or job, or simply to be fashionable.

Since Ancient Egyptian times, hats have been worn as a symbol of authority. Egyptian kings would wear a hat, or crown, showing an asp, a kind of snake, as a sign of their power. Crowns are still worn today by kings and queens. In the past, men used to remove their hats in the presence of women as a sign of respect.

◄ Much of a person's body heat is lost through the head. This fur-lined hat is designed to keep the heat in.

Hats have long been a fashion item and many styles have been designed, including top hats, trilbies, caps and berets. A variety of materials have been used to make them, including silk, felt, straw, fur and, in recent times, even plastic.

▲ A soldier's helmet protects the wearer and tells other people that he or she is a soldier.

LOOK CLOSER

Hats can be designed as purely fashion items that serve no function. Today, some hat makers, or milliners, such as Philip Treacy, are well known for their unusual creations.

Feet first

The earliest types of footwear were sandals or simple shoes made from pieces of leather that were tied around the foot. Over the years, many styles have been introduced to suit different fashions and uses.

Shoes protect our feet from rough surfaces, keep them warm and dry, and make them look good. Some shoes have high heels to make the wearer taller. Varieties of shoes include brogues, sandals, boots, flip-flops and slippers.

◄ Roman sandals were made from a sole of leather or wood that was tied to the foot and leg using leather straps.

In the past, shoes were made of natural materials, usually leather, and created by shoemakers. Today, most shoes are designed on computer and produced by machines. Although leather is still widely used, newer materials, such as plastic and nylon, are also popular.

EUREKA!

During the 1960s, American sports coach Bill Bowerman experimented with a new type of shoe for his athletes. He used lightweight materials and his wife's waffle iron to create the first trainers. He then established what is today one of the world's biggest sportswear companies: Nike.

▲ Film star Cameron Diaz is wearing stylish fashion shoes with thin, pointed high heels known as stilettos.

Fastenings

Next time you get dressed, pay attention to what holds your clothes together. You might use buckles, buttons, zips, poppers or even tiny hooks and loops.

Ancient civilisations used a variety of fastenings to hold their clothes in place. These included pins and brooches to hold togas together and buttons made from shells, bone, wood or pottery. Buckles were sometimes carved with patterns and decorated with jewels.

◀ Buttons are the earliest type of fastening, dating back to **3000** BC.

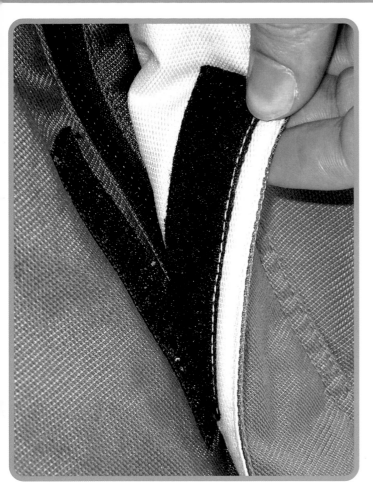

Buttons and pins are still used today to keep clothes on our bodies, but modern technology has given us a few new inventions. These alternatives include Velcro and the zip.

▲ Developed in 1956, Velcro consists of two strips, one with tiny hooks and the other with tiny loops, that cling together.

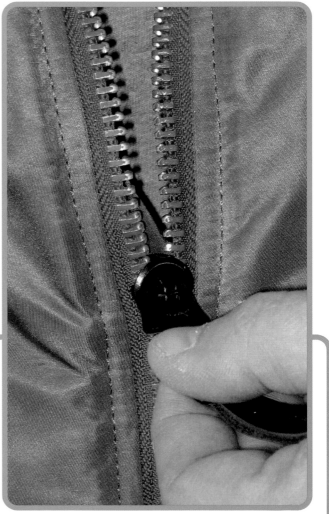

EUREKA!

In 1913, an American engineer called Gideon Sundback designed a sliding fastening device that pulled two rows of teeth together. In 1923, the device was used on a pair of boots and called the zip or zipper. Since then, it has become the world's most popular fastening device.

On the catwalk

Important people have always worn expensive and elaborate clothes to show off their status. They started 'fashions' that others copied. Today, the catwalk is where designers display their latest creations. These new styles greatly influence the fashion industry and the clothes that people wear.

In the past, kings, queens and nobles were the main leaders in fashion, but others, such as politicians and actors, have also had an influence. In the early 19th century, Englishman George 'Beau' Brummell set rules on what men should wear.

◄ George 'Beau' Brummell was able to influence fashion styles thanks to his close friendship with the Prince of Wales, who later became King George IV.

In the 20th century, fashion started to be decided by a few designers. Their creations were worn by film stars or displayed at fashion shows. Due to improved technology, versions of these styles could be available in high-street shops within a few weeks.

◀ At catwalk shows, models wear the latest styles created by top fashion designers.

LOOK CLOSER

Fashion designers can often be as famous as Hollywood film stars. Some of the biggest names over the years include Coco Chanel (shown here), Giorgio Armani, Christian Dior and Gianni Versace. Today, the fashion industry is worth billions of pounds worldwide.

Protective clothes

C lothes can also save lives. Many materials are used to protect people in dangerous jobs, such as firefighters, soldiers, hospital workers and astronauts.

The earliest form of protective clothing was armour used on the battlefield by soldiers. Over the years, armour has been made out of a variety of materials, including thick layers of a natural fabric called linen, as well as leather and metal.

◄ Firefighters need helmets to protect them from falling debris and suits to shield them from high temperatures.

The latest advances in material technology have also helped the development of protective clothing for non-military roles. For example, flameproof materials, such as Nomex, are now used to protect motor-racing drivers.

▼ Spacesuits protect astronauts from low pressure and extreme temperatures. Without them, they would die.

EUREKA!

Developed at the DuPont company by Stephanie Kwolek, Herbert Blades and Paul Morgan, Kevlar is an amazingly strong material – it is five times stronger than steel. This makes it perfect for use in tyres, cables, aircraft panels and in protective armour for the police and armed forces.

Timeline

• c.**5000** BC. The earliest hand-operated looms are used to weave cloth.

• AD **552**. The secret of silk production is smuggled out of China to Europe.

• c.**1800**. The Industrial Revolution begins in England.

• c.**3000** BC. Silk is first made in Ancient China.

5000 BC

• **1764**. James Hargreaves invents the spinning jenny.

• c.**3000** BC. The earliest references to buttons as clothing fasteners.

• c.**4000** BC. The earliest references to skirts and dresses.

• c.**1600**. Suits are introduced as clothing for men.

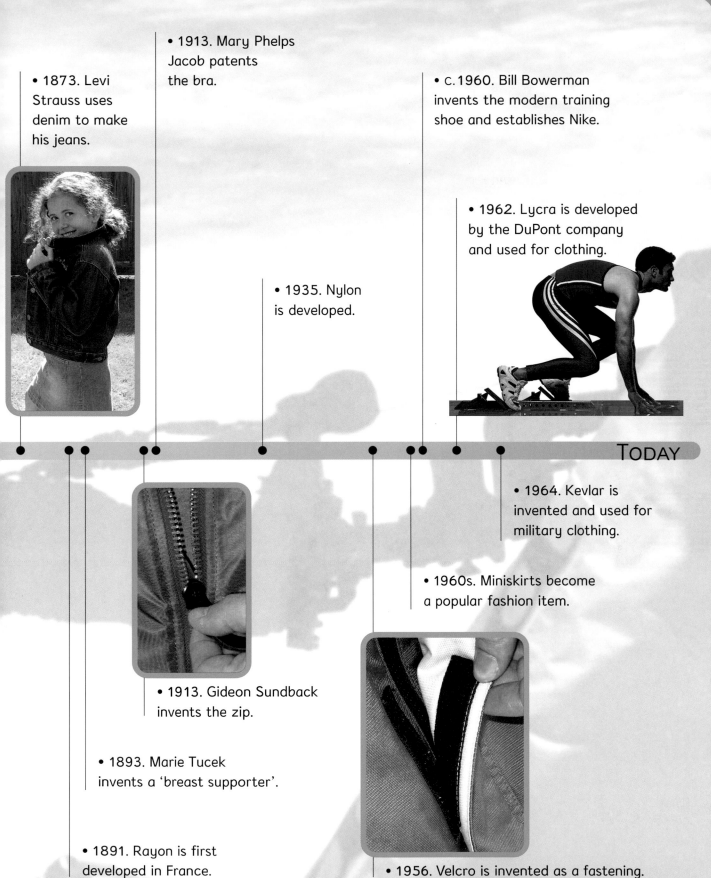

• 1913. Mary Phelps Jacob patents the bra.

• 1873. Levi Strauss uses denim to make his jeans.

• c.1960. Bill Bowerman invents the modern training shoe and establishes Nike.

• 1962. Lycra is developed by the DuPont company and used for clothing.

• 1935. Nylon is developed.

TODAY

• 1964. Kevlar is invented and used for military clothing.

• 1960s. Miniskirts become a popular fashion item.

• 1913. Gideon Sundback invents the zip.

• 1893. Marie Tucek invents a 'breast supporter'.

• 1891. Rayon is first developed in France.

• 1956. Velcro is invented as a fastening.

Factfile

• A pair of Levi jeans that were 120 years old were sold at auction for £33 039, making them the world's most expensive pair.

• Wool was so important to British trade in the Middle Ages that the Lord Chancellor, a senior figure in the government, sat on a woolsack in parliament as a reminder of the nation's wealth.

• The world's largest shirt was made in 2001 and measured 45.4 m long with sleeves that were 15 m long.

• The world's most expensive pair of shoes were made by The House of Berluti based in Paris, France. These pearl-studded shoes were valued at £48 571.

• The tallest pair of high-heeled shoes were called Vertigo shoes and had a heel that measured 40.6 cm high.

• The world's most expensive dress was worn by film star Marilyn Monroe and was sold at auction for £767 042.

• A pair of golf shoes made by Stylo Matchmakers International are the world's most expensive sports shoes. They have ruby-tipped spikes and cost £13 600.

Glossary

Brogue
A sturdy type of walking shoe that is decorated with holes and patterns.

Catwalk
A narrow stage along which models walk during a fashion show to display the latest designs in clothing.

Cocoon
A protective layer that a caterpillar builds around itself. Inside this, the caterpillar changes into a moth or butterfly.

Corset
A stiffened piece of underwear, usually worn by women. It can cover the body from the breasts down to the hips.

Crinoline
A stiff cloth and, later, a framework of metal hoops used in underwear to create wide skirts and dresses.

Dye
A substance that is used to change the colour of something.

Fashion
The popular way of dressing.

Industrial Revolution
A period during the 18th and 19th centuries in Europe and America, when industries, such as cloth-making, began to use powered machines in factories.

Knit
To loop or knot strands of wool together using two needles or a knitting machine.

Loom
A machine that is used to weave threads or yarn into material.

Rayon
A fabric made from wood pulp.

Toga
An item of clothing worn in Ancient Rome made from one piece of material wound around the body.

Weaving
Making cloth on a loom by interlacing lengths of yarn.

Yarn
A long strand of thread that is made by twisting fibres together.

Index